Start Reading
AND TALKING

First Experiences
Going to the Doctor

THE LONDON B
www.bromley.g
Ple

First published in the UK in 2004 by
QED Publishing
A Quarto Group Company
226 City Road
London, EC1V 2TT

www.qed-publishing.co.uk

A Catalogue record for this book is available from the British Library.

ISBN 1 84538 305 2

Written by Ian Smith
Designed by Zeta Jones
Editor Hannah Ray
Photographer Steve Lumb
Models supplied by MOT. With thanks to Gigi.

With thanks to Myatts Field Health Centre and Dr Barbara Cresswell.

Series Consultant Anne Faundez
Creative Director Louise Morley
Editorial Manager Jean Coppendale

Printed and bound in China

Start Reading
AND TALKING

First Experiences
Going to the Doctor

Ian Smith

QED Publishing

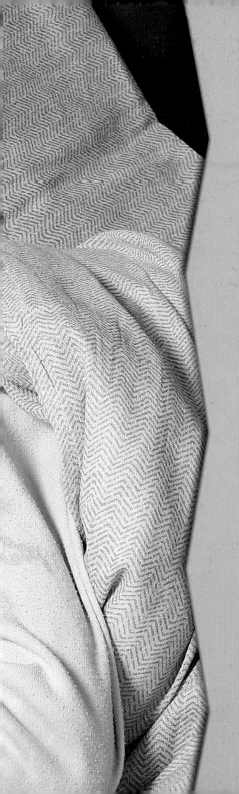

I don't feel well today.

Mum is going to take
me to see the doctor.

5

The doctor is busy.

We have to wait.

I draw a picture for
Mum while we wait.

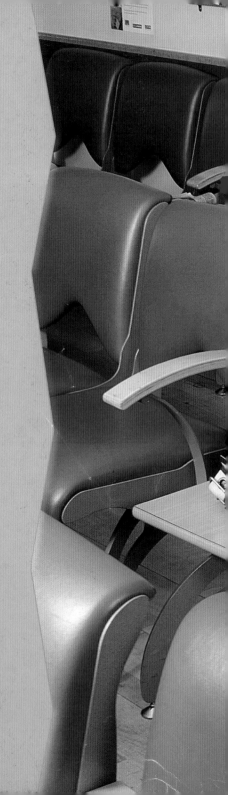

8

The doctor will see me now.

Mum comes with me.

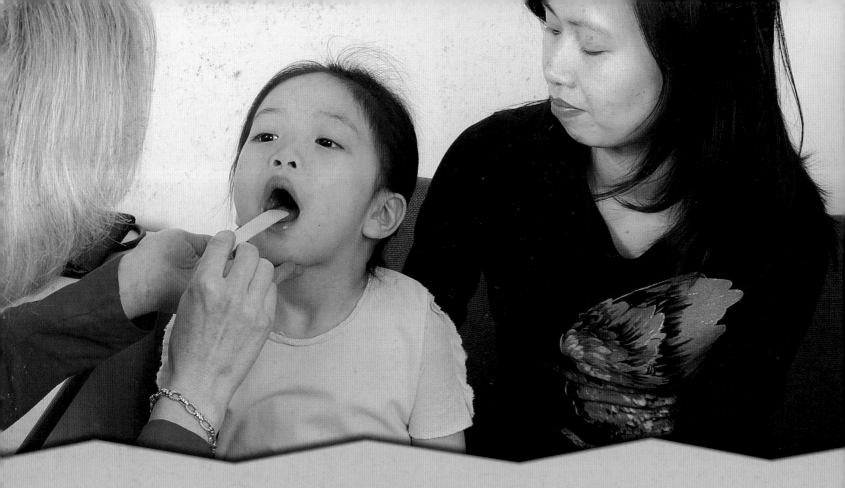

"Show me your tongue," says the doctor. I open my mouth wide.

10

"Now, let me see how hot
you are. This thermometer
will tell me," the doctor says.

11

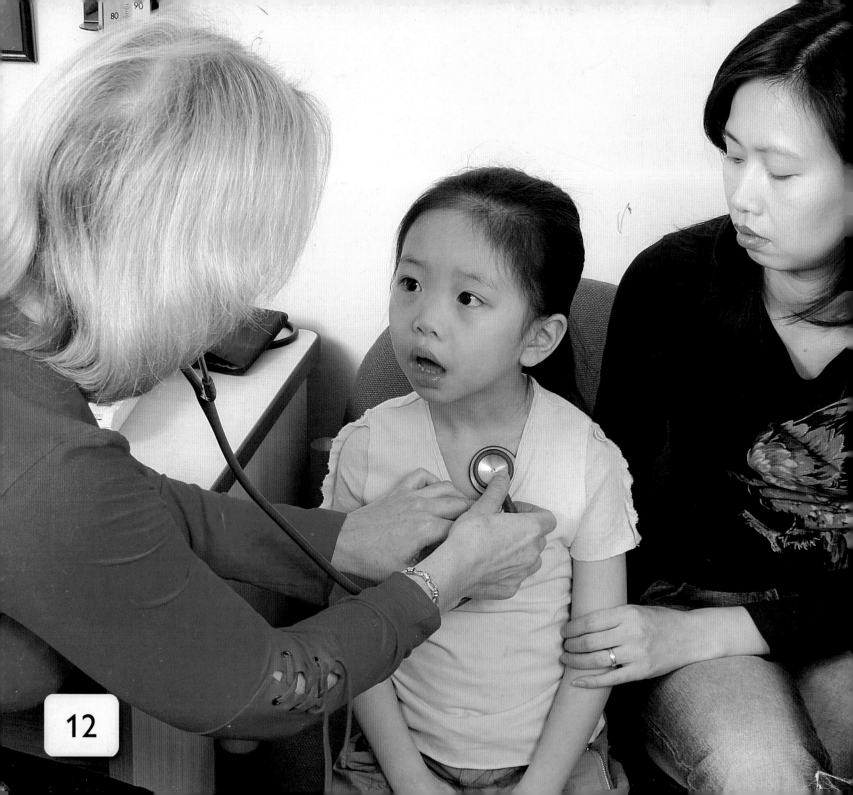

12

The doctor listens to
my chest and my back.

She can hear right
inside me.

The doctor taps
my chest.

She then taps my back.

It feels funny, but it
doesn't hurt.

15

The doctor shines a bright light into my ears.

She looks right inside each ear!

Then the doctor gives
Mum a piece of paper.

The paper says what
medicine I must take.

19

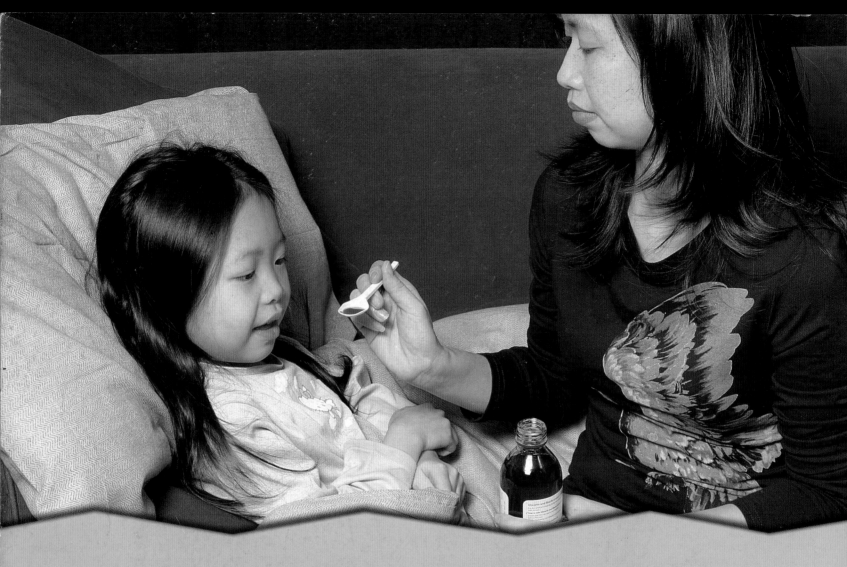

I swallow the medicine from
a spoon. It tastes funny.

Now I am tucked up in bed. Soon I will feel better.

Why did the little girl's mum take her to see the doctor?

Can you remember what the little girl did while she waited to see the doctor?

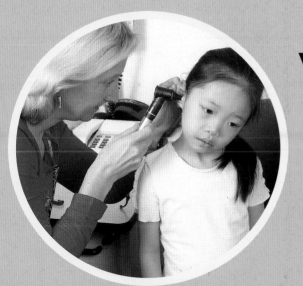

What is happening in this picture?

The doctor gave the little girl's mum a piece of paper. What did it say?

23

Carers' and teachers' notes

- Together, talk about the fact that you often need to see a doctor when you don't feel well.
- Has your child ever needed to visit the doctor? Can he/she remember why? What can your child remember about his/her visit to the doctor?
- Read the book, using your finger to point to each word. Allow time to talk about each picture.
- Re-read pages 6–7. What would your child like to do while waiting to see the doctor? Would he/she take a favourite toy to play with?
- Take turns pretending to be the doctor and the patient, and act out pages 10–17.
- Look at the photo on page 19. Ask your child to name the objects that he/she can see – for example, chair, table, computer. Can he/she spot the small teddy?
- Ask your child to point to the photo that shows the thermometer (page 11). Explain how you often become too hot when you are unwell and that the thermometer shows if you are too hot.
- Together, find the picture that shows the stethoscope (page 12). What can the doctor hear with the stethoscope?
- Explain that the piece of paper that the doctor gives you when you are poorly is called a prescription. Tell your child that you take the prescription to a chemist or pharmacist, who then gives you some medicine or pills to make you better.
- Explain that medicine must NEVER be taken without a grown-up to help.
- Encourage your child to tell you what he/she would do if his/her teddy was poorly. How would your child look after Teddy?
- Help your child to paint a picture of a doctor examining a patient.